DEDICATION

First, this book is dedicated to my family: my wife Julie, and our three children, Paul, Jon, and Sara. Without their sacrifice of time and their encouragement, this book could not have been written.

Secondly, this book is dedicated to my colleagues and to my students at the University of Kansas. My students have been learning "Harmonic Reading" during the past twelve years through hand-out sheets; and the positive feed-back from these students have also been an encouragement to publish this ear-training method.

TABLE OF CONTENTS

FOREWORD

Harmonic Reading is a skill that will supplement melodic sight-singing and dictation skills in all ear-training programs. This system gives the student the experience of singing vertical sonorities -- chords. The student should use this system to aid him in writing down four-part harmonic dictation. It will serve as a "reinforcement process" to this type of learning experience; it will give the student a method to supplement the melodic and rhythmic aspects that normally are taught in an ear-training program.

Harmonic Reading has two pre-requisites for each music student. First, the student must be able to recognize both visually and aurally the seven scale-degrees in both major and minor keys. Secondly, the student must be able to recognize both visually and aurally all the kinds and sizes of intervals that are found in musical scores. If a student has difficulty in hearing and singing melodies with "scale degree numbers," he should practice diligently on these before attempting "harmonic reading." Likewise, if he has difficulty in recognizing a series of intervals as they are played on the piano, or as they appear on a written score, he should drill on intervals before attempting "harmonic reading." This system relies on a knowledge of scale degrees and of intervals in all of the musical examples contained in this book.

When the system of Harmonic Reading is mastered, the student will have a fool-proof method of writing down four-part harmonic dictation. This method gives the student the ability to sing chords that appear on the musical score. It also gives the student a very accurate method of writing down a four-part musical example.

HARMONIC READING

INTRODUCTION

All of the major colleges and universities with schools of music must provide their students with the best possible and the most comprehensive musical training. Music schools design courses to provide the materials and training for all facets and skills necessary for the professional musician. These areas include (1) applied music, or performance skills on one or more instruments, (2) church music, (3) music theory and composition, (4) music education and therapy, (5) musicology, and (6) conducting.

Most music curriculae contain courses that are required for all music majors, irregardless of their major area. These courses include a minimum amount of study in music theory, music history and literature, participation in vocal and instrumental ensembles, instruction in the applied music areas, a proficiency level in keyboard skills, and a certain degree of proficiency in aural skills, i.e. sight-singing and dictation. It is in this last area mentioned that the concern of this method lies -- ear-training. This is an essential skill that all trained musicians must cultivate to as high and as refined a level as possible during their course of study.

What are the specific goals and objectives of an ear-training program? Most courses would include the development in the following skills:
1. Recognition of kinds and sizes of intervals.
2. Recognition of qualities of both triads and seventh-chords.
3. Ability to organize linear pitches (melody) that are constructed from short motives, longer phrases, or complete periods.
4. Knowledge of vertical sonorities (chords) according to the various qualities, and an ability to relate a succession of chords in both functional and non-functional harmony.
5. Cognizance of both rhythm and meter; ability to organize a series of pitches in both symmetrical and assymmetrical meter signatures.

These skills are acquired by the music students through both visual and aural training. In a program of ear-training which includes both sight-reading and dictation, the student's progress is aided by a two-fold reinforcement process. In learning dictation skills, the musical sound(s) is produced and the student learns to notate these sounds (melodic, harmonic and rhythmic parameters) on manuscript paper. In the study of sight-reading, the process is reversed for the student: he sees the written symbols in the score, and "translates" them into audible sounds (by singing, tapping, playing an instrument, etc.)

While sight-reading and dictation in many cases are considered to be separate skills for the music student, a musician must recognize the close relationship between these two skills. A reinforcement process should be present and clearly shown between the two skills, to assist the student as he progresses in each of these two areas. This does not mean, however, that a student who has the ability to sight-read extremely well will automatically possess the skill needed to take musical dictation at a comparable level of proficiency. But it is my belief that the student's progress in both dictation and sight reading should reflect his ability to recognize the correlation between these two skills, and to utilize the reinforcement that is gained from one area of study, and apply it to the other area.

There are presently many textbooks and anthologies available from various publishers that deal specifically with sight-reading skills. Each book may contain original musical examples as well as excerpts from "historical masterworks" of music. The types of examples contained in a sight-reading book are melodies in various types of scales (major, minor, modal, pentatonic, whole-tone, etc.) as well as artificial scales; duets and other small ensemble pieces to be sung simultaneously by two or more students; rhythmic drills, in which pitches are of secondary importance to the rhythmic organization; and often a series of examples dealing specifically with intervals.

Teachers often take their dictation examples from sight-reading textbooks. Areas emphasized in a dictation class may include scale-degree problems, intervals, pitch groups (a series of melodic pitches, either tonally or non-tonally organized), rhythmic problems, and complete melodies (musical phrases and/or periods) that may be harmonically oriented, or which may be outside a key-center entirely.

Dictation is often divided into these two major areas: melodic and harmonic. A music student must be able to relate a series of horizontal pitches that comprise a melodic line; he must also be able to recognize the highest and lowest pitch of this melody, and cultivate recall (tonal memory) of the entire musical phrase in its correct rhythm. Harmonically, the music student must develop the skill to identify a vertical sonority (a chord containing three or more pitches) and to relate it to the preceding and succeeding sonorities. In other words, the student must develop the ability to differentiate between a series of chords that are heard in "functional harmony" (as the chords relate to a tonal key-center) and a series that are "non-functional harmony" (chords that don't relate to a specific key-center).

Ear-training teachers need to develop a method of teaching students to write down sounds as they are played (dictation), both melodic and harmonic. With regard to harmonic dictation, I am unaware of any method that appears in a published textbook. There are perhaps as many and varied philosophies regarding the area of harmonic dictation as there are number of teachers that instruct students in this skill. One method stresses the scale-degree that is contained in the uppermost voice (the soprano) of a chord progression. If scale-degree 5, the dominant, is the soprano pitch, the implied triad in a functional progression would be either the tonic, mediant, or dominant chord. Another method depends upon the particular quality of each chord. If the student hears a minor triad, for example, the chord could be either supertonic, mediant, or sub-mediant in a major key, or it could be a tonic or a sub-dominant in a minor key. These two methods are useful, of course, if the musical examples contain diatonic harmony.

Each of these two methods has advantages as well as disadvantages. Both of these approaches to harmonic dictation are somewhat useful in diatonic harmony in which the chords are functional. However, each of these two methods mentioned would be less useful in a highly chromatic progression or in a non-tonal series of chords.

If a student relies solely on the quality of the chord, or if he attempts to identify the chord by the scale-degree contained in the soprano voice, it may be extremely difficult for him to identify a secondary dominant, a borrowed or altered chord, or to explain a progression in a modulatory section of music.

CHAPTER   I

THE MAJOR TRIAD

CHAPTER I - THE MAJOR TRIAD

Most undergraduate, lower-level music theory courses (freshman and sophomore classes) begin with a study of tertian harmony (chords constructed from intervals of thirds), since the three-hundred year period from 1600 to 1900, often called the "common practice period," is the one most familiar to the college music student. The initial study in an ear-training course that is applicable to tertian harmony, and one which is easily learned by the music student, is one that is dependent upon two and only two important criteria: first, the ability to recognize the SOPRANO FUNCTION; and secondly, the ability to recognize the CHORD QUALITY.

Using the sight-reading approach to this method of Harmonic Reading, that is, one where the student reads from a printed score and "translates" the written notes into audible musical sounds, the process to be followed, may be outlined in the following four successive steps, to be followed in this order:

(1) The student examines the chord, and determines the root of the chord. He first identifies it by letter-name; he then mentally assigns the number "1" to the root of the chord, in whatever voice of the chord the root is located.

(2) The student then looks specifically at the soprano pitch, and identifies what member of the sonority this soprano pitch is (i.e., the root, third, fifth, or seventh of the chord). The student assigns an arabic numeral to the soprano pitch: 1 if root, 3 if the third, 5 if the fifth, and 7 if the seventh of the chord.

(3) The student looks specifically at the three or four pitches contained in the chord and determines the quality of the sonority. If it is a triad, it is identified as a major, minor, diminished or augmented. If the chord is a seventh-chord, containing four different pitches, it is identified as one of the five common seventh-chord qualities: major-major (MM), major-minor (Mm), minor-minor (mm), diminished-minor (dm), or diminished-diminished (dd).

(4) The student memorizes the three number patterns for singing a triad (dependent upon whether the

root, third, or fifth of the chord is in the soprano voice) or one of the four number-patterns for singing a seventh-chord (dependent upon whether the root, third, fifth, or seventh is the soprano pitch). The three patterns for singing triads, where the first number designates the soprano pitch, are 5-3-1 for a root position triad, 1-5-3 for a first-inversion triad, and 3-1-5 for a second-inversion triad. The four patterns for singing seventh-chords will be discussed and illustrated in one of the following chapters.

These three number-patterns are learned systematically; the student begins by singing only the major triad, since this quality triad is the most common one. The following instruction is of utmost importance: the chords are ALWAYS sung in descending arpeggiated form; i.e., the chords are sung in descending manner beginning with the soprano pitch. This is the reason the student determines "soprano function." Another important instruction is this: each chord is sung in closed-structure, and never in open-structure. Therefore, in singing any of the four qualities of triads, the widest interval contained in the arpeggiated chord will be a major sixth.

The system of Harmonic Reading operates essentially in the same manner as does moveable "do" in the solfege method of sight-reading. Using the moveable "do" system, E-flat is "do" if the piece is in E-flat major or minor; D is "do" if the piece is written in either the key of D major or minor. In a similar manner, F-sharp is sung "one" (root) if the chord is the dominant triad in B major or minor (spelled F#-A#-C#). If A-sharp were the soprano pitch, it would be sung "three" (third of the chord) in the dominant triad in key of B major or minor, as would C-sharp be sung as "five" (fifth of the chord). The student first determines what the root of each chord is, and assigns the number "1" to the root. Thus, the numbers used to sing any triad do not in any way reflect a tonal-center in fuctional harmony. The numbers simply identify what chord member appears in the upper voice, (the soprano), and identifies the interval relationship between the numbers which determine the quality of each successive chord.

As the initial process of Harmonic Reading begins, the student memorizes the three number-patterns for singing the major triad. The major triad is the first type of chord to be sung, simply because most of the students will be most familiar with it, as well as the relative importance of the major triad in the tertian harmonic system. As the student begins, using a G-major triad as an example, he will learn the following three positions for the triad: first position, with fifth in the soprano (5-3-1 pattern); second position with the third in the soprano voice (3-1-5 pattern) and lastly, with root in the soprano (1-5-3 pattern). These are illustrated in the following example:

The student should, when first practicing the three number-patterns for the G-major triad, sing each with letter names; the use of letters will solidify in his mind the intervallic relationship between the three members of the chord in each of the three different positions. Thus, the student should begin with the soprano pitch, sing the next two as they appear in "closed-structure" in the score, and then return to the soprano pitch. Returning to the soprano pitch enables the student, when singing a series of triads in a chord progression, to move smoothly from one chord to the next by actually vocalizing the soprano melody. Thus, the student will sing the example above as follows: D-B-G--D, B-G-D--B, G-D-B--G. Initially, the student should check his accuracy of singing by playing the patterns on the piano after he has sung each one. Beware of singing wrong pitches with correct letter-names, or the reverse error, of singing the correct pitches with wrong number-patterns or wrong letter-names. If the system is to be useful the student MUST sing the correct letter names combined with the correct pitches. If either is wrong, the system will make no sense for the student. It is important that when the student is first learning the three "number-patterns" for the major triad that he diligently check his accuracy on the piano. Sing the pattern first; then play it on the piano.

After singing each pattern with letter names, the student couples the correct number-pattern with his letter-names. Using the G-major triad, the student should follow this "thought process:"

    D-B-G--D will now be sung as 5-3-1--5 pattern.
    B-G-D--B will now be sung as 3-1-5--3 pattern.
    G-D-B--G will now be sung as 1-5-3--1 pattern.

The following example illustrates the three positions of the G-major triad, which is followed in each
case by the correct number-pattern by which it should
be sung:

    A review of the process: using the G-major triad,
G is always root, and therefore is always sung with
the number "1" irregardless of what voice it appears
in. Likewise, B is always third, and is sung with
the number "3." And D is always fifth, and is sung
with the number "5." Any time the student sings a
G-major triad in the system of Harmonic Reading, he
will always sing it as illustrated in the example a-
bove. The student then will transpose these three
number-patterns to any other major triad, built on
any scale-degree in any major or minor key. Harmonic
analysis (placing Roman Numerals below the chord) of
the chord progressions which the student sing, will
be discussed in a later chapter.

    Before asking the student to sing the examples of
major triads on the following pages, it is necessary
to discuss the intervallic content of the major triad.
It is very important that the student is aware of the
kind and size of each interval being vocalized; this
knowledge will assist the student to sing much more
accurately.

    Referring back to the three patterns for the G-
major triad, D-B-G in descending form is a root position triad, designated by the numbers $\frac{5}{3}$ in the system
of figured-bass.
    In this root-position, the major third is the lo-
wer third, between B-G; and the minor third appears
between the upper third, notes D-B. Thus, any time a
student sings in descending fashion a minor third

followed by a major-third, the triad is MAJOR.

The next two patterns are called "inversions," since the root "G" is not the lowest pitch. The second triad outlined, B-G-D, in descending form, is a second-inversion triad, in $^6_4$ position, according to figured-bass designation.

The middle pitch is the root, and the lowest pitch is the fifth. The first interval is a major third, between B-G. The perfect fifth between the fifth down to the root, D to G, is now inverted at the octave to become a perfect fourth, G down to D. The descending interval between the outer pitches, B to D, is that of a major sixth, the widest interval that the student will be required to sing for triads.

The third pattern, G-D-B in descending form, is called first-inversion, designated $^6_3$ in the system of figured-bass.

The root is the soprano pitch, and is the first sung. The top interval sung is a perfect fourth, between descending G to D; the lowest interval is a minor third, descending from D to B.

Two more intervallic relationships should be noted as the student begins the process of singing the three number-patterns in the order illustrated, from soprano function 5, to function 3, and lastly to function 1. The first important thing to point out to the student is that when singing the patterns in this order, the last interval of the first pattern, B-G, becomes the first interval of the second pattern; in similar manner, the last interval of the second pattern, G-D, becomes the first interval of the third number-pattern. The following chart illustrates this.

Pattern   5 - 3 - 1 sung as D - B - G - D

Pattern   3 - 1 - 5 is   B - G - D - B

The pattern   1 - 5 - 3 is   G - D - B - G

The second important point which will assist the student is the principle of "inversion at the octave." The most important reason for pointing this out is to assist the student in recognizing the interval between the outer voices, the highest and the lowest.

6

In the 5-3-1 pattern, the interval between 5 and 1 is
a perfect fifth.   In the 3-1-5 pattern, the interval
between 3-5 is a major sixth;   this in the inversion
of the top interval,   5-3, a minor third contained in
the root-position triad. In the third pattern, 1-5-3,
the interval between 1-3 is a minor sixth; this is an
inversion of the lower third, 1-3, found in the root-
position triad.   If the student recognizes that major
intervals invert at the octave to become minor inver-
vals,   and that inverted intervals at the octave add
up to the number nine   (i.e., 6th inverts to 3rd, 5th
inverts to 4th, etc.),   this knowledge will increase
the accuracy of singing the three number-patterns.

    The student   should   now proceed   to practice the
examples   of the major   triads found in the following
pages.   The three number-patterns are reviewed at the
top of the first page of examples;   the soprano function is   given for   the first seven   examples.   Give
yourself the soprano note; sing the triad; check your
accuracy by   playing the   triad on the   piano.   Then
move on to the next triad by singing the soprano note
and repeat the singing process.

8

9

10

11

12

A REVIEW OF THE HARMONIC READING PROCESS

(1) The three number-patterns are always sung as descending arpeggiated triads. After singing the three pitches in a descending order, return to the soprano pitch, so you can move smoothly to the next soprano note and repeat the singing process.

(2) In the three number patterns, the three intervals that the student will sing between any two consecutive numbers will be either the minor third, the major third, or the perfect fourth. Always check your "sung pitches" by playing them on the piano after you have vocalized them. It is important to be accurate.

(3) The student should be aware of the three positions of the major triad as he sings each of them. The 5-3-1 is root position; the 1-5-3 is first inversion, and the 3-1-5 is second inversion.

The student should also note that only in the root position pattern, 5-3-1, will he sing two consecutive thirds; the large interval between the outer two pitches, 5-1, will be a perfect fifth. However, observe that in the two inversions of the major triad the perfect fifth is inverted to become the perfect fourth. Thus, the descending interval between root and fifth, i.e. between 1-5 in the inverted patterns, will always be a perfect fourth.

The student will soon recognize that if the interval of the perfect fourth occurs as the first interval to be sung, that the number pattern is 1-5-3; the first-inversion triad. And if the perfect fourth interval occurs as the lowest interval of the descending triad, the number pattern is always 3-1-5. Thus the perfect fourth always occurs between the numbers 1-5 in the two inverted triad positions.

The student may be assisted in recognizing 5-3-1 pattern as opening three pitches of the National Anthem, "The Star Spangled Banner." He may recognize the 3-1-5 pattern as the "NBC" motive if the pitches are sung, bottom-top-middle order, i.e., 5 up to 3, down to 1. There are undoubtedly other songs for these two patterns, as well as the 1-5-3 pattern that students will recognize, and which songs will aid in remembering each of the three number-patterns.

CHAPTER   I I

The Minor Triad

Singing Major & Minor Triads

CHAPTER II - THE MINOR TRIAD

A minor triad is sung in exactly the same arpeggiated manner as was the major triad. There is only one difference: the quality of the two intervals of the thirds is reversed. The major triad was sung, in descending fashion, by a minor third followed by the major third, in the 5-3-1 pattern. The minor triad is sung with the major third followed by the minor third, in the 5-3-1 pattern. The three patterns will be used in the same manner for all types of triads.

The student should at this point be able aurally to recognize the difference between the larger major third, and the minor third which is a half-step smaller. The major third comprises four half-steps while the minor third contains three half-steps. The student should aurally identify the difference between the major third which inverts at the octave to become the minor sixth, and the minor third, which inverts to become a major sixth.

The next examples will illustrate the method of singing the minor triad in arpeggiated fashion. The student should sing the examples on the following pages in the same manner as he sang the major triads. The "soprano function" is given for the first seven minor triads. Following the examples of minor triads only will be several pages where the examples contain both major and minor triads. Harmonically, this will mean that the student can sing six diatonic triads in major keys (all triads except the diminished leading-tone triad), and he can sing the five commonly-used triads in minor keys (all except the diminished leading-ing tone and supertonic triads). In minor keys, the student will sing examples of both major and minor dominant triads, since both qualities are used with some frequency, dependent on whether the harmonic or the melodic form of the minor scale is used.

The student is encouraged to check his accuracy of pitches by playing each triad on the piano after it has been sung.

18

19

21

22

23

MAJOR AND MINOR TRIADS WITH NON-HARMONIC TONES

The examples on the following pages include both major and minor triads, to which have been added several different types of non-harmonic tones. In these examples, the non-harmonic tones will be written in either the upper or the lower voice. The principle for singing "non-harmonic tones" is this: sing only the non-harmonic tones that appear in the SOPRANO voice, and sing them on a neutral syllable, such as "la." It is unnecessary to sing any non-harmonic tones that may occur in either the inner voices or in the lowest (bass) voice. The pedagogical reason for this is that harmonic reading is always done in descending fashion from the soprano pitch, that the true melodic line can be preserved as a melody. Thus, it is necessary to sing non-harmonic tones in the soprano line on "la" in order that the soprano melody is sung exactly as it appears in the musical score.

The two types of non-harmonic tones used in these examples are PASSING TONES and NEIGHBORING TONES. The passing tones are unaccented; that is, they occur in these examples on half-after a beat. The neighboring tones, sometimes labelled auxiliary tones, may be of two types: the upper neighboring tone, or the lower neighboring tone. Both will be unaccented in these examples, and should be sung on "la."

The following example illustrates these three types (PT. UNT, and LNT) and on the second staff illustrates how they are to be sung.

Soprano functions have been given on the first pages of examples. Sing all soprano notes without a number as a non-harmonic tone, "la." The student will notice that in these examples, all non-harmonic tones occur half-after the beats, not "on" the beats.

25

26

28

HARMONIC READING FROM A SOPRANO LINE

The following pages contain soprano melodies in various major and minor keys. Above each of the soprano notes appears the "function" number, which indicates whether the soprano note is root, third, or the fifth of the triad. Below each of the soprano notes appears a capital letter "M" or a lower case "m" to indicate whether the triad is major or minor, respectively.

This procedure is a reinforcement process of what the student has sung up to this point. On preceding pages, the student has analyzed the printed score, containing three pitches, determined the root of each triad, determined the quality of each chord, and then sung each chord as a descending arpeggio. In the following examples, the student uses the reverse process. He has the soprano melody before him on the score, but will supply the lower two notes of each triad according to the soprano function and quality given for each of the chords. The student may consider these examples a study of how to harmonize a given melodic line.

The first example begins in F major, with a given "A" as the soprano note, which is to function as the third of a major triad. The procedure may be outlined as follows:
1. If "A" is the third of a major triad, the triad will be spelled F-A-C, tonic triad.
2. The number-pattern will be 3-1-5--3.
3. The student may sing by letter names, A-F-C--F, in descending fashion.
4. The student sings the pattern 3-1-5--3.
5. The student checks his accuracy by playing the pitches after he has sung the triad.
6. He moves to the next soprano note (if different from the one just sung) and vocalizes it on "la" before repeating steps 1-5 above, both analytical and aural processes.

As the student sings each successive example, it will become increasingly easier and quicker for him to recognize the letter names, the number patterns, and the actual vocalizing of each chord.

30

31

32

33

CHAPTER   I I I

The Diminished Triad

Singing Major, Minor, Diminished Triads

CHAPTER III - THE DIMINISHED TRIAD

The "diminished triad," which functions as the leading-tone triad in both major and minor keys, (the vii°$_6$) and also the supertonic triad, (ii°$_6$) in minor keys, is sung with the same three number-patterns as are both the major and minor triads.

The diminished triad contains two consecutive minor thirds (for example in descending order, F-D-B as the 5-3-1 position), and contains a diminished fifth (F down to B) between the triad's fifth and root. When singing the 5-3-1 pattern, the student will need to sing two minor thirds in succession. In the other two patterns, i.e. in 1-5-3 and 3-1-5, the diminished fifth will invert at the octave to become the augmented fourth, (for example, B to F, descending.) The diminished fifth and augmented fourth are also referred to as the "tritone," which literally is translated as "three tones" or "three whole-steps."

The examples on the following pages contain diminished triads in context with both major and minor triads as well. When analyzing the functions of the diminished triads, you will note they are either vii°$_6$ or ii°$_6$ triads, and that most of the time they will be written in first-inversion, as the figured bass symbols above have indicated by the subscript "6." Notice that there is only one letter-name difference between the dominant triad (for example, in C major, G-B-D) and the leading-tone triad (in C major, B-D-F) which means that in most instances, these two triads may be used interchangably. The student is encouraged to recognize the difference between the aural sound of each of these two important triads, and the aural effect that each has when preceding the tonic triad at a cadence point in music.

In singing the examples of diminished triads that are written as three-note triads on either treble or bass clefs, it is important that the student realize he will be singing all three number-patterns. This means he will be singing the diminished triad in the unusual root position, the extremely rare second inversion, and the very common first-inversion chord. In chapter V, when four-part chorale style progressions are introduced in Harmonic Reading, the diminished triad will be found in first-inversion (third of the chord in the bass) most of the time.

37

38

39

C H A P T E R   I V

The Augmented Triad
Singing the Four Types of Triads

CHAPTER IV - THE AUGMENTED TRIAD
SINGING THE FOUR TYPES OF TRIADS

The last of the four types of triads to be discussed and sung is the augmented triad. This triad
is defined as containing two consecutive major thirds
and thus it contains an augmented fifth between the
fifth and the root. For example, in 5-3-1 pattern,
G#-E-C is an augmented triad, and the interval of G#
down to C, is an augmented fifth. The mediant triads
in minor keys are often augmented if the harmonic form
of the scale is used, thus raising the seventh scale
degree one-half step from the key signature. In the
key of A minor, the mediant triad could be augmented,
spelled C-E-G#. In major keys, often either the sub-
dominant, dominant, or tonic triad may be augmented.
The typical resolution of an augmented triad is to
allow the raised fifth of the triad to proceed up to
the next scale degree in the key. Thus, an augmented
dominant triad in C major, G-B-D#, will resolve in
such a manner that allows the D# to proceed to E, the
third of the tonic triad.

The following examples contain augmented triads,
in addition to major, minor, and diminished ones. In
these examples, the augmented triad is often preceded
by the major triad spelled with the same three letter
names; for example in the first measure of the first
progression in B-flat major, a Bb-D-F major triad is
followed by a Bb-D-F# augmented triad. This will aid
the student in developing his ability to sing two
consecutive major thirds. After singing the major
triad, the augmented triad follows quite naturally,
being created by simply raising the fifth of the triad by a chromatic half-step.

The augmented triad is the least-used of the four
types of triads, and thus will be the most difficult
to sing, because of its comparatively limited usage.
It is therefore necessary that the student check his
accuracy in singing two consecutive major thirds by
playing them on the piano. Again, as is true of the
other three types of triads, the three number-patterns
remain the same for the augmented triad.

43

45

46

C H A P T E R V

Four-Part Chorale Style

Singing four-voices with non-harmonic tones

CHAPTER V - FOUR-PART CHORALE TEXTURE

The preceding musical examples have been triads written on either the treble or bass clefs. The student has been singing the exact pitches in descending fashion as they have appeared on the staff. There is in actuality, very little music that is written as a succession of triads notated on a single staff. The excercises up to this point have served pedagogically to teach the system of Harmonic Reading.

The remainder of music examples in this textbook are written in "four-part chorale style." A fourth voice, the bass, has been added to the original three notes of the triad, the soprano, alto, and tenor. In four-part texture, where a triad is notated on the grand staff, it is obvious that one of the three notes will be doubled.

The student should apply what he has learned in his study of harmony, chord structure, doubling principles, and chord progressions, to Harmonic Reading. The first examples in this chapter are written in "closed structure," or closed-position. This term is defined as the four-voiced chord in which the upper three voices are adjacent chord-tones. There will always be the distance of less than an octave between the soprano and tenor voices. For example, if the soprano note is A, and it is the third of the triad, the 3-1-5 pattern, the alto will sing "F" a third below the soprano, and tenor will sing middle "C," the fourth below the alto. There is the interval of a major-sixth between the soprano "A" and tenor "C." The three number-patterns that the student has learned have each been in closed structure; the widest interval sung has been a major sixth. The only difference you will notice in the next examples of four-voiced chords, is that the third pitch in descending order, that is, the tenor note, is now notated on the bass clef. In singing closed structure, you will sing the soprano, alto, and tenor voices in the exact order as they appear on the grand-staff, just as you did in the preceding series of triads.

At this point in the learning process, it is not necessary to sing the bass voice. It is important at this point, that the student mentally identifies the pitch of the bass voice, because this note determines the position of the chord, and will therefore affect which one of the upper three voices will be doubled. The student should sing only the soprano, alto, and tenor voices in the order that they appear (i.e., in closed structure). Continue to check your accuracy by playing the three pitches on the piano after you have sung the chord. Do not write in the soprano function numbers in these excercises; make this a mental process, rather than a written analytical project. In this way, Harmonic Reading will give you more facility and accuracy in your analysis and singing from the musical score.

51

52

53

54

CLOSED, NEUTRAL, AND OPEN STRUCTURES

Two additional part-writing structures are now added to the preceding "closed structure" chords. It is necessary to have these additional methods of constructing a chord because of vocal range and because of chord position, (i.e., root position, first inversion, and second inversion.)

NEUTRAL STRUCTURE is defined as a triad, written in four-voiced texture, that has the soprano note doubled by the tenor exactly one octave lower. There is, therefore, always a perfect octave between the soprano and tenor voices in neutral structure. This structure is used mainly for triads in first inversion.

Neutral structure requires an additional step in the process of HARMONIC READING. It requires that the student mentally rearrange some pitches before singing the triad in descending fashion with one of the three number-patterns. There will be one pitch absent from the triad in the three upper voices, because the soprano and tenor voices are singing the same letter-name, an octave apart. Study the following series of four-part triads, including five in first inversion, and three (marked with an asterisk) in neutral structure.

EXAMPLE CONTAINING THREE NEUTRAL STRUCTURE TRIADS

In the second triad, the pitches are C-F-C, reading from the soprano down to the tenor. The student must place the missing pitch from this F-major triad, the note "A," between the top two voices before he sings C-A-F to the number-pattern 5-3-1. In the next triad marked with an asterisk, the student analyzes the chord as a G-Bb-D chord; he places the missing note, "B-flat," between the alto "D" and tenor "G" in order to sing it as G-D-Bb, the descending 1-5-3 number pattern. In the third measure, the chord marked with an asterisk is the dominant triad; the student will again place the missing "E" between the alto "G" and the tenor "C," and will sing descending C-G-E, to the pattern 1-5-3.

The student should note that, in this example, the first-inversion triads have been scored with the soprano note doubled; this is the most common doubling procedure for first-inversion triads. The student should note that where he must insert the missing pitch, the soprano function is either 5 or 1. If the soprano function is 3, as in the third chord in the first measure, the soprano pitch has already been doubled by the bass; in this case the triad will never appear in neutral structure, and no insertion of a missing pitch will ever be necessary.

OPEN STRUCTURE is defined as a four-voiced triad that is written with more than one octave distance between the soprano and tenor voices. It is impossible for most students to sing a triad in open structure, since it would require in many instances more than a two-octave range. Therefore, just as the student did in neutral position, he must transpose one of the tenor or bass pitches up an octave, and insert it between the soprano and alto pitches. In some instances, it is necessary to transpose two pitches and place them between the one-octave distance that is between the soprano and alto pitches, (as in the second chord in the next example.)

The student should study the following example, which contains triads in open structure (marked with an asterisk *) as well as in neutral structure.

EXAMPLE CONTAINING OPEN & NEUTRAL STRUCTURES

In the first triad in this example, the student
analyzes it as a tonic triad, with the third, "A," in
the soprano. In order to sing it in the closed structure 3-1-5 pattern, the student must transpose the
note "F" up and place it between the soprano and alto.
Likewise, in the third triad, a sub-dominant triad in
the 1-5-3 pattern, the tenor "F" must be transposed
up one octave, and sung between the soprano and alto
pitches. In the second triad, the soprano and alto
are one octave apart; the student analyzes this as a
tonic triad in the 5-3-1 pattern. In this chord, two
pitches must be transposed and placed between the top
two voices -- the bass "A" and the tenor "F." The
student is asked to follow the same procedure for the
remainder of open-structure triads.

The student is again reminded of this important
method of singing chords in Harmonic Reading: always
sing each chord in CLOSED structure, thus necessita-
ting the transposition of one or two pitches. In
the next examples, figured-bass symbols will be given
below each chord to aid you in your analysis process.
Neutral structure is used only for first-inversion
triads; both closed and open structures may be used
for root position and second-inversion triads.

57

60

61

63

CHORALE-STYLE WITH NON-HARMONIC TONES

The following four-part chorales contain passing-tones and neighboring tones, as was true in preceding examples written as 3-note triads on a single staff.

Continue to sing the non-harmonic tones in the soprano voice on a neutral syllable, such as "la." You will notice the presence of a passing-tone or a neighboring tone in the alto, tenor or bass voices, but you will not be asked to sing them.

A passing-tone is used to fill in the interval of a third in any of the four voices, thus forming a conjunct melodic line in that voice. A neighboring tone (also labelled "auxiliary tone") will move upward or downward by step, and then return to the original pitch once again. A very common passing-tone is one which form the seventh of a chord, a "passing seventh." This is indicated by arabic numerals 8-7 in a root position triad, a by numerals 6-5 in a first - inversion triad. Once again, these passing-tones are to be sung ONLY if they appear in the soprano voice.

There is an exception to the typical doubling principle that applies to a triad in four-voice texture. Occasionally, a triad is constructed with its fifth omitted; this means that either the root or the third of the chord is doubled, or occasionally the root may be tripled. In these cases, the student mentally supplies the missing fifth of the chord (which will either be in 3-1-5 or 1-5-3 pattern, and never of course, in the 5-3-1 pattern for obvious reason), places it in its proper position in one of the two number patterns, and sings the chord as a complete triad.

65

67

69

CHAPTER VI

Seventh-Chords

Singing the Five Common Sevenths

The Bass Function: Chord Position

Singing all types of Non-harmonic tones

CHAPTER VI - SINGING SEVENTH-CHORDS

Beginning with this chapter VI, one more pitch is added to the triad, forming a seventh chord that contains four different letter-name pitches. The first type of seventh chord to be sung is the major-minor seventh chord. The first word, "major" refers to the quality of the triad, for example, G-B-D. The second word, "minor," refers to the quality of the seventh. In this type of sonority, the interval between the root and seventh as a minor-seventh, for example G-F. Thus, the chord G-B-D-F in root position is known as the "major-minor" seventh chord, which most often functions as a "dominant seventh," the V_7 chord.

The student learns to place the fourth pitch in relationship to the three pitches of the triad; he learns the seventh-chord patterns by thinking of them as expansions of the triad patterns. Think of adding the seventh to the triad through the following process:

1. Root Position: the 7th precedes the existing 5-3-1 pattern, forming 7-5-3-1 pattern. This, reading in a descending order, consists of three 3rds: m^3 plus m^3 plus M3 intervals.

In the three inversions of the major-minor seventh chords, the number "7" ALWAYS follows the number "1," since the minor seventh, 1 up to 7, inverts to become the major second, 7 up to 1. Thus, the pattern 7-1 in descending order becomes 1-7 when it inverts at the octave.

2. First Inversion: the third of the chord is in the bass; the triad pattern was 1-5-3. Place the 7th after the root, thus forming the 1-7-5-3 pattern.

3. Second Inversion: the fifth of the chord is in the bass; the pattern for the triad was 3-1-5. Insert the 7th following the root, to form the new 3-1-7-5 pattern.

4. Third Inversion: the seventh of the chord is
in the bass. The triad pat-
tern used for 3rd inversion
is the 5-3-1; add the 7th of
the chord following the root,
forming the 5-3-1-7 pattern.

The following chart indicates in vertical form
(as the patterns are sung, in descending order from
the soprano pitch) exactly how the seventh-chord number patterns evolve from the three triad-patterns:

Root Pos....		. 1st INV....		..2nd INV...		. 3rd INV.	
TRIAD	7th	TRIAD	7th	TRIAD	7th	TRIAD	7th
	7 F	1	1 G	3	3 B	5	5 D
5	5 D		7 F	1	1 G	3	3 B
3	3 B	5	5 D		7 F	1	1 G
1	1 G	3	3 B	5	5 D		7 F

On the first page of musical examples containing
the Mm7 chord, the "evolution process" of the chart
above is illustrated on the staff, with an A-major-
minor seventh-chord, A-C#-E-G. The soprano functions
are given for several examples; figured-bass symbols
have also been provided to assist you with your analysis of each chord. Sing the pitches of each chord in
descending fashion; return to the soprano note; move
to the next soprano note, and repeat the process.
Continue to check your accuracy by playing the chords
on the piano after you have sung each one.

EXAMPLES:

7531 - 7

5 3 1 7 - 5

3 1 7 5 - 3

1 7 5 3 - 1

74

75

77

78

79

IDENTIFYING THE POSITION OF THE CHORD:
THE BASS FUNCTION

Up to this point in the process of Harmonic Reading, the student has been singing each chord as a descending arpeggio from the soprano note, returning to the soprano note, and moving to the next for a repetition of the process. The position of the chord up to this point has not been identified through the singing process. Figured-bass symbols have provided written analysis for the position of the chord, and the student has been encouraged to make a mental analysis of the chord progression in each example.

From this point on in the process of Harmonic Reading, the student will continue to sing each chord in descending fashion, but will now add three more vocalized pitches after he has sung one of the number patterns. After the chord has been arpeggiated, and the student has returned to the soprano pitch, he will vocalize "soprano-bass-soprano" pitches. Just as was true of the pitches of each chord, the student will sing the bass pitch with one of four specific numbers: 1 for root position, 3 for first inversion, 5 for second inversion, and 7 for third inversion.

For example, consider a C-major triad scored with "G" in the soprano, and "E" in the bass, in neutral structure ("C" in alto, and "G" in the tenor). The student will sing down from the soprano 5-3-1--5, after which he repeats the soprano "5," then sings the bass "3" and returns to the soprano pitch "5." In other words, the complete process is 5-3-1--5, 5-3-5.

By adding the last three numbers after the chord has been arpeggiated, the student vocally identifies the complete vertical sonority as to the function of the soprano pitch, the quality of the chord, and the position of the chord, by identifying the function of the bass voice. This procedure is repeated for each successive chord; a non-harmonic tone in the soprano voice is sung on "la" before moving to the next chord.

The student should carefully study the following example. This contains a series of seven chords in B-flat major. The top two staves, (grand-staff) illustrate the written progression; the third staff contains the arpeggiated version of each chord in the progression, and indicates to the student how each is to be sung. Sing these chords several times before proceeding to the examples on the following pages. The most important advice to each student at this point is to be very accurate. If the student sings "3" for a bass function, for example, he must be certain that the chord is in first inversion. He must also be certain his pitch is accurately vocalized. In other words, the student must be careful to sing the correct pitch with the correct number-pattern.

82

84

85

SINGING THE MINOR-MINOR SEVENTH CHORD

There are four additional seventh-chords that need explanation. In the following group of musical examples, the minor-minor seventh chord is used. The major-minor consists of a major triad and a minor seventh above the root of the chord. The intervals, from the root up, are M3 plus m3 plus m3. The minor-minor seventh chord can be explained as a derivation from the Mm7 chord, by lowering the third of the triad one half-step. This reverses the quality of the two types of thirds; the minor-minor seventh chord contains intervals of m3 plus M3 plus m3, reading upwards from the root. For example, the major-minor seventh chord spelled C-E-G-Bb, becomes minor-minor when the third is lowered: C-Eb-G-Bb.

Minor-minor seventh chords are the supertonic, mediant, and sub-mediant seventh-chords in any major key; and they are the tonic and sub-dominant sevenths in minor keys. They are found in all four positions and are sung with the same four number-patterns used for the major-minor sevenths. The student is reminded that, when singing the three number-patterns for inversions, the minor third inverts to become a major sixth, just as the major third inverts at the octave to become a minor sixth. And the minor seventh inverts to become a major second, that always appears between 1-7 in the descending number-patterns.

89

91

93

SINGING MAJOR-MINOR (Mm7) and MINOR-MINOR (mm7) FROM A SOPRANO MELODY

The following musical examples are to be sung from a soprano melody, to which has been designated the soprano function and one of five chord qualities: M, m, or d triads, or Mm or mm for seventh-chords. There will be no chord "position" designated in these examples by figured-bass symbols, because there is no written bass-line. The student will, therefore omit singing "soprano-bass-soprano" numbers following each of the chords. The student will sing the correct number pattern for one of the three triads or one of the two seventh-chords, return to the soprano note, move to the next soprano note, and repeat the singing process for each successive chord.

The student may consider these examples as a process of harmonizing a given soprano melody. A soprano note, in either a major or minor key, has at least four possible functions: root, third, fifth, or seventh. Likewise, each soprano note may be a part of at least five chord qualities, listed above. Thus, the chord vocabulary is greatly expanded, especially when the diatonic scale-degrees are altered, which is true in many of the musical examples. The student is able to analyze each chord by thinking of the letter names that match the number-patterns, and is able to place a Roman Numeral beneath each of the chords. Roman Numerals will now be used for several different types of chords: diatonic chords, secondary dominants, borrowed chords, and pivot chords that function in a modulation.

Undoubtedly, the student's singing is more accurate in both pitch and correct number patterns. However, it is still advisable for the student to check pitches by playing each chord on the piano after it has been sung.

95

97

98

COMPLETION OF THE SEVENTH-CHORD VOCABULARY

There are three types of seventh-chords to be both classified and identified, which will complete the seventh-chord vocabulary. These are the major-major, the diminished-minor, and diminished-diminished seventh-chords.

The major-major, (designated by two capital letters, MM7), may be considered an expansion of the major-minor seventh chord. In each case, the triad is major; but in the MM7 chord, the seventh is raised a half-step to become the major-seventh. The intervals contained in the MM7 chord, reading upward from the root, are M3 plus $m3$ plus M3. This chord is found as a tonic or sub-dominant seventh-chord in major keys, and as a mediant or sub-mediant seventh chord in minor keys. The number-patterns are identical to those used to sing the Mm7 and the mm7 chords.

The diminished-minor, (designated by two small, lower-case letters, dm7,), is also known as a half-diminished chord. It is built, from root upwards, of a $m3$ plus $m3$ plus M3 intervals. The half-diminished seventh chord functions as leading-tone seventh in major keys, and as a supertonic seventh in minor keys. It is often found as a secondary leading-tone seventh chord in chromatic harmony.

The last type of seventh chord is the diminished-diminished chord (designated dd7) which is also known as the fully-diminished seventh-chord, since both the triad and the seventh are diminished. Reading from the root upwards, this chord contains $m3$ plus $m3$ plus a $m3$. For this reason, the fully-diminished chord is both symmetrical, since adding another $m3$ would be the root, and also aurally ambiguous. It is difficult for the student to ascertain the function of a dd7 merely by its sound, because theoretically any of the four pitches may function as the root of the chord. The function of this chord (roman numeral) may only be determined by looking at the musical score. This fully-diminished chord functions as the leading-tone seventh in minor keys, as well as a secondary leading-tone seventh in chromatic harmony. For example, a dd7 spelled F#-A-C-E$^\flat$ is the vii^{o}7° of G minor; it would be a vii^{o}7°/V in the keys of C minor or C major.

99

The following chart illustrates the intervallic content of each of the five types of seventh-chords:

QUALITY	DESIGNATION	THREE THIRDS		
Major-Major	MM 7	M_3	m^3	M_3
Major-minor	Mm 7	M_3	m^3	m^3
minor-minor	mm 7	m^3	M_3	m^3
dimin-minor (half-dimin.)	dm 7	m^3	m^3	M_3
dimin-dimin (fully-dimin.)	dd 7	m^3	m^3	m^3

The following musical examples contain all four types of triads and all five types of seventh-chords. The student should continue to stress accuracy of both the number-patterns and the pitches. Analyze each of the chords mentally, as quickly as possible, for quality and roman numerals. There are passing-tones and neighboring-tones in the examples.

103

104

106

108

SINGING TRIADS, SEVENTH-CHORDS, And NON-HARMONIC TONES

The next group of musical examples contains all types of triads and seventh-chords, and the following non-harmonic tones:

1. UPT and APT - unaccented and accented passing tones.

2. UN and LN - upper neighbor and lower neighbor tones.

3. SUSP - suspensions; three common ones are the 9-8, 7-6 and 4-3 that occur in soprano, alto, or tenor voices; the 2-3 (also called 5-6) that occurs in the bass voice; the change of inversion (change of bass) suspension; and the change of harmony, (change of chord) suspension.

4. ESC - the escape tone (also called eschapee,) (approached step, res. by skip)

5. APPOG - the appoggiatura tone; (approached by skip; resolved by step.)

6. ANT - the anticipation tone; (approached by either step or skip, resolved as a repeated note.)

7. RET - retardation tone; essentially it is a suspension that resolves in an upward direction.

As the student was previously instructed, he is to continue singing non-harmonic tones on a neutral syllable, such as "la." The passing tones and neighboring tones contained in the soprano voice should be sung as before. The student should use one of the following methods of singing the five remaining non-harmonic tones:

1. The student can, at the point of suspension, sing the suspended note on the sullable "la." Using the first musical example in the key of F major, the student sings the first chord a major 3-1-5-3, 3-1-3. The second chord, the dominant, contains a 4-3 suspension in the alto voice, pitch F before it resolves to pitch E. The student may sing the chord on beat three "5-la-1-7-5," where "la" is the vocalized suspended note F. This is followed by singing the chord on beat four, which contains the resolution note E as

109

"5-3-1-7-5, 5-1-5." Using letter names, the student sings the pitches "G-F-C-Bb-G" with "F" being the suspended note in the alto, and then sings the pitches on beat four, "G-E-C-Bb-G" where "E" is the resolution note. In this first method, the student vocally identifies both the suspended note "la" and the note of resolution, as an arabic numeral 3, 6, or 8, the chord tone.

2. The student may elect this second method of dealing with non-harmonic tones in Harmonic Reading. He will sing the first tonic chord in the first musical example in the usual manner: 3-1-5-3, 3-1-3. The student may then mentally analyze the second chord containing the suspension, and may verbally state it contains a "4-3" suspension in the alto. He will sing only the chord that contains the resolution note, pitch E. In this second method, the student ONLY sings chord tones. Thus, he will analyze only the chords on beat three; he will sing the chord on beat four, "5-3-1-7-5, 5-1-5."

Either of these methods is a valid approach to learning Harmonic Reading. Each student should elect the option that he feels will give him the best understanding of non-harmonic tones. The first method may be called the "vocal approach," since the student sings the non-harmonic tones on "la," and the chord-tones with the appropriate chord number. The second method may be referred to as an "analytical approach" since in this method, the student does not sing the non-harmonic tones, but only verbally analyzes them as to the type, and in which voice they appear.

The student will also treat the remaining non-harmonic tones in the same manner as he does in dealing with the suspensions.

111

112

113

114

115

116

CHAPTER VII

Non-Functional Harmony

CHAPTER VII - NON-FUNCTIONAL CHORD PROGRESSIONS

All of the preceding musical examples were written in a "key;" there may have been modulations within any of the measures of each of the examples, or the musical example may have ended in a key different from that in which it began. But each of the examples was tonal. Scales used in these examples included the major and minor diatonic scales as well as the chromatic scale, found in most music of the nineteenth century.

The following pages of musical examples are not written in a "single tonality," or necessarily in a "key." They may or may not imply modulations. The examples are often nothing more than a series of major or minor triads that relate by root movements of seconds, thirds, tritones, rather than the more conventional fourths or fifths of tonal music. Cadences are not the traditional authentic, half, plagal, or deceptive; rather the concluding two or three chords are often root-movements by ascending seconds or by descending seconds. Often, the most significant change between the final two chords will be the result of a chromatic minor-second; for example, a G-B-D chord may be followed by an E-G♯-B chord, which in turn may be followed by a C-E-G chord. This involves using the pitch G-natural moving to G-sharp, and then back to G-natural again in one of the voices. If the chromatic change is in the same voice, (i.e., alto), it is a chromatic inflection; if each of these two pitches appears in different voices (for example, the G-natural in the alto, followed by the G-sharp in the soprano), it is referred to as a "cross-relation."

Sing these tertian structures in the same manner as you sang the examples written in functional harmony. Use the same three or four number-patterns for each of the triads or seventh-chords, respectively. Return to the soprano pitch after you have outlined the triad as a descending arpeggio, and move to the next soprano note. Continue to check your accuracy of pitch by playing the chords on the piano after you have sung them. It is very easy for the student to "stray from the printed score" in all these examples, since there is no tonic note or chord ("home base" so to speak) around which an entire progression revolves.

121

122

123

124

126

127

0-8191-324